ESPELUCATE PA' PEINA' TE

WILD WEST

ALEJANDRO CASTRO

Foreword by Johan Gotera
Translated from the Spanish
by Arthur Malcolm Dixon

$\mathcal{A}$
$\it{'Alliter}$atïon

WILD WEST | ALEJANDRO CASTRO
Translated from the Spanish by Arthur Malcolm Dixon
First edition in English in October 2023

www.thealliteration.us

Design by Elena Roosen
Cover by Andrea Martínez
Proofreading by Tess Rankin & Félix García
Editorial Coordination by Amayra Velón

ISBN: 979-8-9876541-3-2

PROLOGUE

Harsh, cruel, and ironic, the poetry of Alejandro Castro stands for a provocative space of reflection at a time when poets tend toward the pomp of self-promotion and the ceremonies of public display. His memorable foray into controversy, *Un-Letter to a "Young" Poet(?)* (2015), shook up high-minded society. This work's very title, with the acrimony of a criminal summons, questions the pedagogical transmission through which the gifts of poetry must supposedly—and effortlessly—circulate. But Castro distances himself from that conciliatory lineage, choosing instead to explore the catastrophe of the everyday and to conceive, all for himself, a niche within public space from which to question, from a place of anger or desire, the plotlines of the historical present.

In *Wild West* he explores unprotected civic space, the neglect produced by a state that has, dangerously, absented itself from the city. From this vantage point, he meditates on the destruction wrought by the breakup of social accords. The city, it seems, is dead; now, the periphery is all there is. Born of a nonrestorative disillusionment, the poetic voice takes shape as the dweller-in-evil who points out the love, the stench, and the noises of this urban horizon. Here we cross paths with the "aspiring murderer," the neighbor who "lunges at his wife," and the body waiting for its worms.

"Let others sing the unbroken greatness / of being poor and good / I know how much violence fits into two days," he tells us in a poem whose title, "The Torrid Zone," ironically rewrites a tradition annulled by the bonanza of death. This torrid zone that once delineated territorial pride has turned into an absurd shade of local color, where the celebrations of the living are shaded by a canopy of violence. The time for sermons is over, he declares, and thus it seems now is the time for the body. The dilemma between the bodily and the spiritual is debated in the poem "03-02," which takes place on the third floor of some building or another in the wounded city. Divided by a hallway, two voices sense each other, mutually, in their respective solitude: "Across the hallway lives a witch / who has spent her life wondering / which heaven sends the sax down on Sundays / so much baffling jazz to set the scene / for conjuring." On the other side, the tenant who completes the scene perceives, "transparent from / her door the obscenity of ash / from candles lit to who knows which / virgin suicides."

Here we see, apparently, the distribution of good and evil. But, beyond a cultural reading endorsing or condemning either of these subject's morality, the poem puts forth a definition of country that situates the politics of the body as a response to the outcry of faith. If the witch's practices presuppose worship, altars, and veneration, then jazz—which shares an ethnic component with traditional *brujería*—prefigures, on the contrary, a return to bodily reality, setting a scene in which the body senses its own density through a listening experience that serves as both incitement to nomadism and anticipation of sexuality. This is not a pursuit of consolation through faith; it is, rather, the bodily execution of sound as an exercise of desire and a withdrawal of the subject into its own materiality.

Setting body against spirit, the poet addresses the distance that separates the spiritual submission implied by all worship from the need to extemporize the personal journey of the body—be it individual or social—driven by desire or necessity to discover its own political potentiality. From a literary point of view, this means making of writing an earthly vocation, and from a civic point of view, it means reconsidering the subject's relationship with power, bringing about a consequent breakdown of the cult of personality that, through paths similar to those of superstition, infects political citizenship. "There is no better description of our homeland / than the five infinite feet between your / door and hers: in my country / heaven and hell are neighbors / infecting each other like on the third floor." So the poem ends, with a nod toward the generalized contamination of civic space and the insurrection of evil in everyday life.

Both of this poem's *persons*, upon exiting their private domains, will inevitably enter into the disorder of the real, the unprotected realm, the places the poet explores: "under bullets over city." There, the *antipatriotic* slander that could be read in the alien (for some) sign of jazz will be negated by the all-equalizing violence the poet senses as an "age of iron."

But the questioning of the spiritual is, at its root, a critique of the devout body and of the worship of power in any and all forms. Jazz, urban wanderings, sexuality, and crime are just some of the exercises through which the body uncouples itself from historical grandiloquence. In this sense, Alejandro Castro seeks to alter the national epos and the disfiguration of the symbolic plot with which power tells its own tale. He reveals other ways of belonging to the city, and he exposes the asymmetry between the citizen and the rantings of historical discourse. In his "Song for Bolívar," through small doses of blasphemy, he advances his critique of the stridency and artifice of the Bolivarian Olympus: that subjective space that renders the citizen a worshiper and builds a state cult recurrently validated by the glories of the past.

We are, the poet says, in the age of iron: the age of "gunshots and merengue," where there is no sense in expecting favors from any given deity. His refutation of heroes demands that we pull political relationships down from Olympus, reconfiguring them outside of rituality, among the ungodly. To that end, the poet proposes a convulsive eros and forces beyond the norm with which to answer back to the myth of the state. "Your name," he tells Bolívar, "is an alibi, / a bill plucked from the mud, worthless, / yet another busted square"; "the only glory in your name, Liberator, / is a street of clacking heels / size twelve."

The connotation of this shoe, strutting onto the scene of heroism, could not be more disruptive. It represents a disproportion that cannot be placidly contained by any symbolic mold. It points toward a principle of reality with which to empty out history and dissolve absolute values. Poking its way in, a mere foot, it calls to mind some ruined statuary that once upheld the rituals of faith. But the *travesti* body that traverses the extensive redlight district of Caracas expects neither attention nor favors. Instead, it is hurled into the space of violence, about to be destroyed, inasmuch as it is a body in jeopardy. This body thus encapsulates our affections and our fears. Its starkness recalls, in turn, the monstrosity of Flora—with her big feet and high heels buckling under her excess—in the poem by Virgilio Piñera, the gay Cuban writer who faced his own revolutionary age with the same anger.

With all its irreverence, this *twisted* heel impinges upon epic discourse and unmakes the plot of identity, entering into a scene of gendered (and generic) mutation: a scene from which regulatory identifying information, such as the face, has been flagrantly extracted, rendering it a meaningful omission, displaced from the poem's field of vision.

The *man's* foot that violently dwells in the space of *the woman* recalls, nonetheless, a greater discomfort that could be extrapolated to the storyline of generalized violence. At the same time, the wayward, disproportionate heel that crosses the nominal space of heroes (Avenida Libertador) ironically undermines the logic of *great men* and opens the door to irregularity as a sign with which to shake down the oppressive mechanics of homogenizing morality.

Thus the lascivious, the grotesque, the fall from grace of immolated heroes and the eruption of an oppositional eros, along with the substantiation of a shared decadence, make up the angle of starkness and neglect from which certain urban subjects view and suffer history. This angle, free of institutional tale-telling, is the area of critical practice that Alejandro Castro's poetry privileges. From this vantage point he asks moral questions and faces—through an aesthetic open to all present-day stimuli—the effects of the euphoria that made ash of political possibility under the imperatives of redemption and the pressures of utopia.

Johan Gotera

WILD WEST

ALEJANDRO CASTRO

for Martha Millán

a Martha Millán

A QUIEN PUEDA INTERESAR:

qué haces ahí sentado al final de la página
qué quieres del poema

acaso un nombre que bautice tu fracaso
   un viaje más allá de toda frontera
una palabra al fin perdurable

piensas que aquí hay verdad o belleza
una clave un templo un camino
otro mundo ahora que estás cansado
de mirar una mirada nueva
para posarla sin miedo en lo mismo
un mundo a secas

qué quieres del poema
que te acompañe de noche
que duerma contigo / que se vaya contigo
que te lleve con él
que diga qué del pasado   de la lengua
del país

quieres patadas   te gusta duro el poema
te gusta dócil en cambio te gusta sabio
atrevido moderno qué   qué buscas aquí
la ciudad o el sol   una experiencia
un modo una fosa una voz
al final de la página
qué.

TO WHOM IT MAY CONCERN:

what are you doing sat there at the end of the page
what do you want from the poem

maybe a name to dub your failure
    a trip beyond all borders
a word at last enduring

you think there is truth or beauty here
a key a temple a path
another world now that you're tired
of looking   a new way to look
fearlessly at the same old thing
a world cut and dry

what do you want from the poem
should it spend the night
should it sleep with you / should it come with you
should it take you with it
what should it say about the past   or language
or the land we come from

do you want kicks do you like the poem rough
or do you like it docile or perhaps you like it wise
daring or modern what   what are you looking for
city or sun   experience
a way a grave a voice
at the end of the page
what.

CASALTA
CASALTA

Upon you, birds
of the unending lands,
I sought a space for so much death.

Sobre vosotras aves
de las regiones infinitas
busqué un espacio para tanta muerte.

José Agustín Goytisolo

CASALTA

Tengo que sobrevivirte
entre los perros que de madrugada
profieren la música del odio.
Debajo de las balas encima de la ciudad
día tras día Casalta tengo que sobrevivirte.

Pero te llevo conmigo Casalta irremediablemente
con pañales en el balcón y las aceras
tu alegría impostada y el ruido de los dientes en el frío
o quizá en el miedo de cerrar la puerta
y que por sus resquicios entre la jauría
los disparos y el merengue
como si no te importara deforestarte siempre
y encender los bombillos que regala el gobierno
para olvidar.

Quiero dejarte aquí Casalta en el poema
tapiarte con los escombros de la infancia.

Yo —mi hermano y yo— adivinando
el color de los carros en que mi padre no vendría
inventando canciones de apagón
sobreviviéndote milagrosamente
detrás de las rejas.

CASALTA

I've got to survive you
in amongst the dogs at dawn
who sing the songs of hate.
Under bullets over city
day after day Casalta I've got to survive you.

But I bear you with me Casalta come what may
with diapers on the balcony and sidewalks
your feigned joy and the sound teeth make in the cold
or could it be in fear of closing the door
and the dog pack the gunshots and merengue
infiltrating through the cracks
as if you did not mind being forevermore deforested
and turning on the government-handout light bulbs
to forget.

I want to leave you here Casalta in the poem
brick you up in childhood rubble.

Me—my brother and I—guessing
the color of the cars in which my father was not coming
making up songs for the blackout
surviving you miraculously
behind the bars.

EL PESO DE LA SANGRE

a Javier

Voy a escribirte despacio
como si no quisiera morir mañana.
Aquí de este lado del mundo
el reloj tiene agujas.

Nada sé de la vida niño
salvo que es más hermosa
cuando abres esos tremendos
ojos tuyos como una sentencia.

Malgasto aquí un poema
para pedirte no para implorarte
en nombre del peso de la sangre
que no te parezcas a mí.

En nada nunca.

Escupe a quien te diga
que somos iguales.

Hazte lejos de mí
y tu vida será como la mía
cuando abres esos tremendos
ojos tuyos que hicieron una casa
de mi bruno corazón.

THICKER THAN WATER

for Javier

I'm going to write you slow
as if I didn't want to die tomorrow.
Here on this side of the world
the clock has hands.

I know nothing of life my boy
but that it is more beautiful
when you open those terrific
eyes of yours like a sentence.

Here I waste a poem
asking you no begging you
in the name of stuff thicker than water
do not be like me.

Ever at all.

Spit on anyone who tells you
we're the same.

Be far away from me
and then your life will be like mine
when you open those terrific
eyes of yours that made a home
of my pitch-dark heart.

CENTRO PLAZA

antropólogos
historiadores del arte
profesores de literatura
¿quién podrá traducirle
al colega del futuro
el aroma inaudible del
"haz patria mata un gay"
"Robertico lo mama bien"
"dile no al comunismo"
tanta poesía garabateada
primitiva en las paredes
del pasado?

CENTRO PLAZA

anthropologists
art historians
literature professors—
who will translate
for future colleagues
the inaudible odor of
"save ur country kill a gay"
"Robertico gives good head"
"say no to communism"
so much poetry scrawled
primitive on the walls
of the past?

HORADAR LA TIERRA

a Adalber Salas

1
Bienaventurados los gusanos
porque de ellos será el reino
de mi cuerpo: carne para nadie.

2
Bienaventurados los pobres
porque no sabrán nunca
que detrás de la montaña
sigue el mundo
tal como lo conocemos.

3
Bienaventurados los poetas
porque ellos horadarán
la tierra.

DEMERIT THE EARTH

for Adalber Salas

1
Blessed are the worms
for theirs will be the kingdom
of my body: flesh for no one.

2
Blessed are the poor
for they will never know
behind the mountain
this world carries on
just as we know it.

3
Blessed are the poets
for they will demerit
the earth.

TOY STORY

Lo recuerdo: me miraba
altanera desde la cima
de un G. I. Joe.

No pude matarla.
Aquella caja
no era su ataúd.

Recuerdo el día que descubrí
una   cucaracha
en el baúl de los juguetes

y supe que era tiempo
de crecer.

TOY STORY

I remember: it was looking at me
stuck-up from the peak
of a G.I. Joe.

I couldn't kill it.
That box
was not a coffin.

I remember the day I discovered
a   cockroach
in the toy chest

and knew it was time
to grow up.

EL DÍA DESPUÉS DE LOS ENAMORADOS

a Verónica

Me pregunto qué hacen los chinos con
tanto corazón rosado cada quince
de febrero. Si algún sótano alberga
los cadáveres de la vendimia, alimento
para ratas que nada saben de economía
sumergida y todo a cincuenta meta la
mano el día después de los enamorados.

Tal vez las abejas de peluche puedan libar
flores de plástico y cada quince de febrero
haya una orgía de conejos y gatitos
ebrios de vino barato.   Quizás
si aquel cura supiera en qué devino su hazaña
si tuviera que leer mil veces gracias con ese
y contemplar filas interminables
frente a hoteles mugrientos sin amor
habría ardido con fruición en la hoguera
del Imperio cada quince de febrero.

THE DAY AFTER VALENTINE'S

for Verónica

I wonder what the Chinese do
with so many pink hearts every February
fifteenth. If some cellar houses
the dead bodies of the vintage, food
for rats who don't know underground
economy and half off can't miss
these deals the day after Valentine's.

Maybe the stuffed bees can suck
on plastic flowers and every February fifteenth
there is an orgy of bunnies and kitties
drunk on garbage wine.   Perhaps
if that priest knew the outcome of his deed
if he were forced to read a thousand times *luv u*
and contemplate unending lines
outside filthy loveless motels
he would have been happy to burn at the Empire's
stake every February fifteenth.

CANTO A BOLÍVAR

Ahora que todo lleva tu nombre, Bolívar,
y no es una metáfora,
vamos a poner las cosas en su sitio.

A Miranda no lo mató el bochinche sino tú.
Y Colombia se hizo grande ahíta de miserias.
Y el Olimpo que levantamos,
en alabanza   para que tú reinaras,
es una barriada interminable.

Y ahora,
que te ha dado por resucitar o reencarnar,
no hay un alma que no sea alérgica
a tu nombre y eso, Bolívar,
tampoco es una hipérbole.

Tu nombre es una coartada,
un sucio billete que nada vale,
una plaza cualquiera repetida,
una esquina.

Tu nombre es un país sin mar,
el pico más alto de la cordillera más pobre / del planeta.

La única gloria en tu nombre, Libertador,
es una avenida sonora de tacones
talla cuarenta y seis.

SONG FOR BOLÍVAR

Now that everything has your name on it, Bolívar,
and that's no metaphor,
let's put things in their place.

Miranda did not die of bochinche—you killed him.
And Colombia grew greater gorged on misery.
And the Olympus we raised up
in praise   that you might reign atop it
is one endless slum.

And now
you're into coming back to life or reincarnating
not one soul is unallergic
to your name and that, Bolívar,
is no hyperbole.

Your name is an alibi,
a bill plucked from the mud, worthless,
yet another busted square,
a corner.

Your name is a landlocked country,
the highest peak of the poorest range / on earth.

The only glory in your name, Liberator,
is a street of clacking heels
size twelve.

LOS ÚLTIMOS CINCUENTA

a Gina Saraceni

Yo era un dios a los cien metros
todo zancadas poderosas
en los pulmones por primera vez aire
no humo.

Yo era un dios a los doscientos metros
primerísimo lugar engreído victorioso
primerísimo en algo al fin.

A los trescientos metros
nadie podía detener el tren que yo era
el avión más rápido del mundo.
Podía sentirlo:
     algo detrás de mí se quedaba
partía yo corriendo del pasado.

Era la hora de la venganza (ráfaga fugaz)
alzado en hombros adolescentes pletórico de deseo
sumergido en la marea de pecas transpiradas
y Caracas desaparecía a los trescientos cincuenta metros
olvidada en mi vuelo incontenible minúscula
desde el podio imaginado.

La muerte me sorprendió entonces
en los últimos cincuenta agazapada
detrás de la recta final en cada paso
una pena las piernas iban solas hirviendo
los ojos sin el mundo la mueca de dolor
el cuerpo atropellado por una ambición
superior a sí mismo

THE LAST FIFTY

for Gina Saraceni

I was a god at a hundred meters
all powerful strides
my lungs filled for the first time with air
not smoke.

I was a god at two hundred meters
very first place big-headed triumphant
very first place at something at last.

At three hundred meters
no one could stop the train I was
the fastest airplane in the world.
I felt it:
    something being left behind me
I went running from the past.

It was the time of vengeance (fleeting flash)
lifted on teenage shoulders brimming with desire
sunk in the tide of sweaty freckles
and Caracas disappearing at three hundred fifty meters
forgotten in my unstoppable flight tiny
from the imagined podium.

Death surprised me then
at the last fifty crouching
behind the home stretch at every step
sorrow legs going on alone boiling
eyes without the world grimace of pain
body bowled over by an ambition
greater than itself

33

humano cuerpo
sin alas ni turbinas.

Estoy cansado
vivir es una carrera de cuarenta y dos
kilómetros y agoté la alegría en trescientos
cincuenta metros.

human body
no wings no turbines.

I am tired
life is a twenty-six-mile
race and I ran out of happiness in three hundred
fifty meters.

NAVIDAD

Es temporada de renos
en Caracas. Temporada
de pinos de verdad
tan hermosos
que parecen de plástico
y pinos de plástico
tan hermosos
que parecen de verdad.

Lo bello siempre parece
de otra especie
de otro mundo:

por eso es tan hermosa
Caracas
en navidad
por los renos
extraviados y la nieve
bajo el sol absoluto

por las luces en el Guaire
y la cruz del norte / vacía
tan lejos

de Israel.

CHRISTMAS

It's reindeer season
in Caracas. The season
of real pine trees
so beautiful
they look plastic
and plastic pine trees
so beautiful
they look real.

Beauty always looks to be
a different kind
a different world:

that's why Caracas is
so beautiful
at Christmastime:
the straying reindeer
and the snow
under absolute sun

the Guaire lit up
and the northern cross / empty
so far

from Israel.

CARIBE

De todos los monumentos
construidos por el hombre
mi favorito es el mar.

CARIBBEAN

Of all monuments
built by man
my favorite is the sea.

LA ZONA TÓRRIDA

debí nacer burgués
para amar a los pobres de la tierra
debí dormir arrullado por la voz
de una nodriza redonda
debí nacer en París

para encontrar poesía en todas partes
y confundir con deseo la mirada curiosa
del aprendiz de asesino
para pensar que la batalla que cada noche
retumba en mis oídos
se libra en nombre de alguna causa digna
y mirar las luces en el cerro
maravillado

que otros canten la grandeza indómita
de ser pobre y bueno
yo sé la violencia que cabe en dos días
perrea mami perrea

mi infancia huele a borracho
a morcilla sancochada en las aceras
el vecino embiste contra la mujer
a ella le gusta la gasolina
avienta desperdicios por la ventana
sube el volumen a la radio
cómo le encanta la gasolina
sube el volumen al televisor
y cada sábado es sen-sa-cional

en el barrio todos los días hay fiesta
todos los días hay muerto

THE TORRID ZONE

I should have been born bourgeois
so as to love the poor of the earth
I should have been lulled to sleep by the voice
of a plump wet nurse
I should have been born in Paris

to find poetry in everything
and misread as desire the curious look
in the eyes of the aspiring murderer
to think the battle that echoes
in my ears every night
is fought for some just cause
and look at the lights on the hillside
in awe

let others sing the unbroken greatness
of being poor and good
I know how much violence fits into two days
perrea mami perrea

my childhood smells of drunk
of blood sausage parboiled on the sidewalk
the neighbor lunges at his wife
a ella le gusta la gasolina
litters out the window
turns the radio up
cómo le encanta la gasolina
turns the TV up
and every *sábado* is *sen-sa-cional*

in the barrio every day a party
every day a dead body

todos los días alguien se orina sobre la belleza
que anda sarnosa dando lástima
     perreando.

every day somebody takes a piss on beauty
looking mangy pitiful
      perreando.

NIGÉRRIMA

dicen que era una mujer hermosa
Porlamar aullaba a su paso
las palabras más sucias
sin conmover uno solo
de sus ciento ochenta centímetros

dicen que abandonó a sus hijos
que un brujo enamorado
convocó a todos los elementos
y la llevó más allá del mar

regresó cuando el vientre le dolía
dicen ése que diez veces abierto
todavía clamaba furibundo

regresó con gusanos en los pies
por regresar dicen pero ella sin asco
altiva como era hermosa regresó

ahora
yo no sé qué decirle su voz arrugada
me mira sabe que pienso el poema
y posa   posa y me mira
sabe que los gusanos vuelven por
su carne y sin asco los espera soberbia
con toda la belleza que le queda.

EBONY

they say she was a gorgeous woman
as she walked past Porlamar howled
the dirtiest of words
and could not touch a single foot
of her six

they say she left her kids
a witch doctor in love
summoned the elements
and carried her beyond the sea

she came back when her belly hurt
they say her belly ten times split
was still crying out incensed

she came back with worms in her feet
cause she came back they say but she undisgusted
aloof and gorgeous as she was came back

now
I don't know what to say to her
her wrinkled voice
sees me knows I am thinking this poem
and poses   poses and sees me
her voice knows the worms are coming for
her flesh and undisgusted she awaits them prideful
with all of the beauty she has left.

LA CIUDAD DE ARCILLA

Llueve. A cuántos va a matar
esta vez el barro. Cuántos
van a morir de noche
cuando la casa se les venga encima.
Aquí el miedo no persuade
a nadie. La galerna no acalla
el sarao ni calma la sed.
Llueve. Y la ciudad no es más
hermosa sino más temible.
No hay poetas en los bares
cuando llueve. No hay cristales
para verla resbalar como lágrima.
Las almas se amontonan
se aglomeran en las salidas del metro
guarecidas de la lluvia mientras llueve
en la ciudad de arcilla. Cientos.
Miles. A cuántos va a llevarse la vaguada.
Cuántos van a morir de lluvia. Quién
abrazado a la nevera.

CITY OF CLAY

Rain. How many will the mud
kill this time. How many
will die by night
when the house caves in.
Here fear persuades
no one. The gale neither silences
the soiree nor sates thirst.
Rain. And the city is not
prettier, it is more frightening.
There are no poets in bars
when it rains. There is no glass
to watch it slide down like a tear.
The souls stack up
they bunch together at the metro exits
safe from the rain while it rains
on the city of clay. Hundreds.
Thousands. How many will be taken by the riverbed.
How many will die by rain. Who
hugging the fridge.

ORTOGRAFÍA

Subiendo a la Simón hay un cartel:
"prohibido votar basura".

Se trata de un error más o menos
frecuente entre los consumidores del idioma.
"Votar" y "Botar" no es lo mismo
aunque parezca arbitrario. Las palabras
homófonas —maldito prefijo griego—
son un dolor de cabeza.

El tráfico no avanza. Miro el cartel
y pienso que conspiran. Los errores
no existen ni las casualidades. Señoras
y señores: "prohibido votar basura".

SPELLING

Right where you hit La Simón there is a poster:
"prohibido votar basura."

This is a relatively
common error among language consumers.
But "votar" and "botar" are not the same
although this may seem arbitrary. These words,
homophones—damn that Greek prefix—
can be a real pain in the neck.

Traffic is at a standstill. I glance at the poster
and think this is a conspiracy. Errors
do not exist, nor do coincidences. Ladies
and gentlemen: "prohibido votar basura."

LA PEQUEÑA BALLENA

a Joaquín Marta Sosa

No sé cuántos versos tiene este poema
o si merezca llamarse así no quiero
contar las sílabas de este verso
preguntarme si es moderno
o experimental.

Escribiré la tarde para que quede escrita
para que alguien alguna vez sienta su ruina el sonido
de las motos a lo lejos el olor
a tabaco de mis manos los gritos
que sabotearon la siesta el vallenato   durísimo
de unos vecinos a los que tampoco
interesa cuántos versos tiene
este poema.

THE BABY WHALE

for Joaquín Marta Sosa

I do not know how many lines are in this poem
or if it deserves to be called that I do not want
to count this line's syllables
wonder if it's modern
or experimental.

I will write the evening so it's written down
so someone someday feels its ruin the sound
of far-off motorbikes the smell
of tobacco on my hands the screams
that sabotaged the siesta the blaring   vallenato
of the neighbors who likewise
don't care how many lines
are in this poem.

BELLAS ARTES

Él tenía una cicatriz en el rostro.
Me preguntó si vivía en Los Magallanes:
"Tú te pareces al chamo que mató
a un hermano mío". Él señaló en su bolso
una pistola. Yo tenía un libro de Coetzee.
"¿Me parezco al que mató a tu hermano?"
No miraba la pistola sino la cicatriz.
Pensé: ¿luciré como él mañana?
"Tú vives en los Magallanes", ya no era una pregunta.
Su acento era una cicatriz: una huella de animal
en el cemento. Quise decirle que nunca
he estado en Los Magallanes, que hace tiempo que
vivo como en una burbuja, pero él estaba seguro:
"Tú te pareces al chamo que mató a mi hermano".
Alcancé a decir "no", aunque no era una pregunta.
"Yo lo que voy es armado". Su aliento era una cicatriz:
algo muerto en lo vivo. Luego se fue dando tumbos.
Pensé: esta también es La edad de hierro.

BELLAS ARTES

He had a scar on his face.
He asked me if I lived in Los Magallanes:
"You look like the dude who killed
my brother." He showed me a gun
in his bag. I had a Coetzee book.
"I look like the guy who killed your brother?"
I was staring at the scar, not at the gun.
I thought: "Will we look alike tomorrow?"
"You live in Los Magallanes." It was no longer a question.
His accent was a scar: an animal track
on cement. I wanted to tell him I have never
been to Los Magallanes, for some time now
I haven't really left my bubble, but he was sure:
"You look like the dude who killed my brother."
I blurted out a "no," but it was not a question.
"I'm tooled up." His breath was a scar:
a dead thing on a living thing. He lurched away.
I thought: this too is the *Age of Iron*.

ARMAGEDDON

> Ubi solitudinem faciunt pacem appellant

Nos prometieron un diluvio
una guerra. Dijeron que todo
terminaría que no tendríamos
aire para respirar que cuando
cayeran las bombas ni las ratas
sobrevivirían. Una debacle
nos prometieron. Dijeron
que el océano iba a tragarse
a las ciudades y los árboles
como furias nos perseguirían
en la noche de los tiempos.

No resultó tan fácil acabar
con todo. Cayeron las bombas
demasiado lejos. Hay demasiado
aire. Da lo mismo un árbol
que una piedra. Hay demasiadas
ratas. Demasiados hombres.
Nada pudo tragarse a las ciudades.
Todo fue demasiado. Nada pudo
con todo. Nos quedamos con las
manos en la cabeza. Se nos llenaron
de polvo las latas de atún en el refugio
atómico.

Ven, meteorito iracundo.
Yo te espero. Ven
danos una paz que dure.

ARMAGEDDON

Ubi solitudinem faciunt pacem appellant

They promised us a flood
a war. They said it all
would end we'd have no more
air to breathe and when
the bombs fell not even the rats
would make it. They promised us
catastrophe. They said
the ocean was to swallow up
the cities and the trees
come lurching after us like furies
in the nighttime of all time.

But it was not so easy ending
everything. The bombs fell
too far off. There's too much
air. A tree's no different
from a rock. There are too many
rats. Too many men.
Nothing could swallow up the cities.
It was all too much. Nothing was up
to everything. We stood there with our
mouths agape. Our cans
of tuna in the bomb shelter covered
in dust.

Come, wrathful meteor.
I'm waiting. Come
give us a lasting peace.

PÉREZ BONALDE

Todos van borrachos en el autobús
borrachos pero contentos.

Caracas ahí estás toda herida
toda rota insultando odiando.
Caracas ahí estás tus cloacas
abiertas tus calles cerradas
tus multitudes sordas
y el calor.

¿Cómo se llama la montaña
que te niega el mar?

Caracas toda penuria la maldita
circunstancia de estar rodeada de
montañas sin nombre y la pobreza
te mira no te abandona no te deja
mirar la pobreza en todas partes un estruendo
un asesino un rancho
un montón de basura.

Yo saco la cabeza por la ventanilla
y el olor a mierda me indica
que estoy en casa.

PÉREZ BONALDE

Everybody on the bus is drunk
drunk but happy.

There you are Caracas hurt all over
broke all over hurling insults hating.
There you are Caracas your sewers
open your streets closed
your multitudes deaf
and the heat.

What's that mountain called
that keeps you from the sea?

Caracas all shortage the goddamned
circumstance of being surrounded by
nameless mountains and poverty
is looking at you never leaving you behind
never letting you look poverty everywhere a crash
a murderer a shack
a pile of trash.

I stick my head out the window
and the shit smell tells me
I am home.

REDACCIÓN

a Anaira Vázquez

Según el periódico
durante el fin de semana
"veintisiete muertos violentos
ingresaron a la morgue
de Bello Monte".

Válgame Dios.

COMPOSITION

The paper says
over the weekend
"twenty-seven dead
—all violent—
were sent to the Bello Monte morgue."

My God.

03-02

a Guillermo Vargas

Frente a tu puerta vive una bruja
que ha pasado la vida preguntándose
de qué cielo viene el saxo los domingos
tanto jazz incomprensible para ambientar
el conjuro tanto blues tanto Satchmo
rudo en el estruendo de los dedos
que convocan a la muerte.
En el infierno se escucha el cielo.

A ti también te llega diáfana desde
su puerta la obscenidad de la ceniza
del velón encendido a quién sabe
qué vírgenes suicidas.

Nada describe mejor a la patria
que el infinito metro que separa tu
puerta de la suya: en mi país
el cielo y el infierno se avecinan
contagiados como en el piso tres.

03-02

for Guillermo Vargas

Across the hallway lives a witch
who has spent her life wondering
which heaven sends the sax down on Sundays
so much baffling jazz to set the scene
for conjuring such blues such Satchmo
gritty in the clacking of the fingers
summoning death.
Heaven is audible from hell.

It finds its way to you as well transparent from
her door the obscenity of ash
from candles lit to who knows which
virgin suicides.

There is no better description of our homeland
than the five infinite feet between your
door and hers: in my country
heaven and hell are neighbors
infecting each other like on the third floor.

EL HUMO Y LA LIBERTAD

Salven a las ballenas niños que lo demás no importa
y nadie sabe a ciencia cierta a qué animal pertenece
el cuerno de África.

Maldigo mi tiempo cien por ciento
libre   de humo.

Es verdad la humanidad es una plaga
salven a los toros a las focas salven el Amazonas.

Yo maldigo y defiendo con los dientes manchados
mi derecho a morir.

SMOKE AND FREEDOM

Save the whales kids nothing else matters
and no one knows exactly which animal grows
the Horn of Africa.

I curse my time, one hundred percent
smoke   free.

It's true the human race is a plague
save the bulls the seals save the Amazon.

I curse and uphold with stained teeth
my right to die.

REVOLUCIONES

1

Camaradas
la poesía
es culpa del capitalismo.

2

Camaradas
(de noche)
casi todos los gatos
son pardos
y a los ojos
de los gusanos
todos los cuerpos
son bellos.

3

Camaradas
Marx
ha muerto.

4

Camaradas
no es sueño
la vida
no es juego
la vida
no es una.

No tiene memoria
    el pueblo
    tiene hambre.

REVOLUTIONS

1
Comrades
poetry
is capitalism's fault.

2
Comrades
(at night)
almost all cats
are gray
and in the eyes
of worms
all bodies
beautiful.

3
Comrades
Marx
is dead.

4
Comrades
life
is not just a dream
is not just a game
life
is not just.

The people
    don't remember
    they are hungry.

FUNCIÓN DE LA POESÍA

las palabras mágicas no estaban en latín
ni en alguna muerta lengua prehistórica
las palabras mágicas las que podían hacer
que mi mejor amigo amarrara las trenzas
de mis zapatos o me dejara columpiar
en su cuerpo eran las mismas que dirigía a la maestra
enfurecida para explicar que la del siete
no sería tabla de salvación.

por eso a mi poesía le falta poesía
porque la gracia verbal aparece
tan sólo frente a la duda de un potencial
columpio porque irrumpí en el templo
profanándolo y la belleza
para mí es un medio y la poesía un cebo
a veces un escudo como cuando jugaba con mi nombre
porque no salía el poema y decía alejo
yo alejo y castro.

FUNCTION OF POETRY

the magic words were not in Latin
nor in some dead prehistoric tongue
the magic words the ones that made
my best friend tie my shoes
or let me swing
on his body were the same I'd say to our infuriated
teacher to explain the seven times table
won't keep us above water.

this is why my poetry lacks poetry
because my eloquence comes
only in response to hesitance
from a potential swing because I burst
into the temple and profane it and beauty
is a means to an end and poetry is bait
sometimes a shield like when I used to play with my own name
because the poem wasn't coming and I'd say yo alejo
I castro.

CONTRAPUNTEO VENEZOLANO DE LAS MISES Y EL PETRÓLEO

> En el mundo hay todo tipo de cosas
> que funcionan como espejos.
> JACQUES LACAN

salvo una   ellas son blancas
él no

ellas son asexuadas
tránsfugas del deseo

él en cambio (también)
es un símbolo fálico

ellas no tienen nada en la cabeza
un moño a veces

él puede matar de hambre y fuego
a todos los pelícanos del mundo

una cubana paga por ellas

un gringo paga por él

los maricos del gobierno
quieren ser como ellas

los maricos de la oposición
también

ellas creen

VENEZUELAN COUNTERPOINT: PAGEANT QUEENS AND OIL

All sorts of things in the world
behave like mirrors.
JACQUES LACAN, TR. SYLVANA TOMASELLI

all but one of them   are white
he's not

they are asexual
runaways from lust

he on the other hand (likewise)
is a phallic symbol

they have nothing on their minds
a bun sometimes

he's capable of killing every single pelican
on earth with fire and hunger

a Cuban woman pays for them

a gringo man for him

the government fags
want to be just like them

the opposition fags
do too

they believe

que la enfermedad holandesa
se cura con antibióticos

viene la ronda de preguntas
temida ronda
qué triste pasa
qué triste cruza
por el televisor

en una noche tan linda
como ésta, dime,
¿qué es negro por dentro
necio por fuera?

the Dutch disease
is cured with antibiotics

and now the questions round
that dreaded round
passes so sadly
so sadly across
the TV screen

on a night as pretty
as tonight, tell me,
what's dark on the inside
and dim on the outside?

CRUISING

Este dolor es raro.
No se aloja en mi cuerpo,
es también mi cuerpo
perdido entre la gente
que miro y me mira y no sé
qué piensa de mí cuando me mira.
Yo soy distinto: nadie sospecha
que no debería estar aquí
porque no brillo ni hago brillar
la baranda que me salva del
abismo. ¿Me salva? Puedo acabar
con todo ahora. Estoy aquí, sin embargo,
soporto mi cuerpo porque quiero.
Si pudiera decirlo todo.
Hay un tipo que me mira.
No sé qué piensa o por qué
me mira o si me mira porque sus ojos
están en mí. Los ojos casi siempre
están abiertos, sin mirar.
Sólo yo me obligo: estaré atento
a este suelo escupido, el bigote
del tipo que ahora se acerca.
Tanta fealdad sin cadena.
Lo que me quiere es robar,
que es como decimos aquí:
lo que quiere es robarme.
La primera fórmula es sin lugar a dudas
más interesante. Nada llevo de valor.
Apenas mi vida que de valer
no vale.

CRUISING

This pain is strange.
It's not lodged in my body,
it too is my body
lost among the people
I look at who look at me
and who knows what they think
of me when they're looking at me.
I'm different: nobody suspects
I shouldn't be here
since I do not shine nor do I shine
the handrail that saves me from the
abyss. It saves me? I could end
it all right now. I'm here and still
I bear my body's weight because I want to.
If only I could say it all.
This guy is looking at me.
I don't know what he is thinking, why
he's looking at me or if he is looking
at me since his eyes are on me. Eyes
almost always open, without looking.
I alone force myself: I'll stay alert
to this spit-covered floor, the mustache
of the guy approaching now.
So much unchained ugliness.
He's tryna jack me
which is how we say:
he means to rob me.
The first formula is doubtless the
more interesting. I have no valuables.
Only my life, and that is not worth jack.

LIKE A PRAYER

Por ese entonces yo tenía un novio
que cantaba canciones de Madonna
y no sabía
si quería ser drag queen
poeta o domador de palomas.

Talento le faltaba
para casi todos esos oficios
y otros que rondaron
su avara cabecita hueca
dormida en mi pecho.

Cuando atentaron en París
un trece de noviembre
Madonna estaba de gira
y ya mi novio se había largado.

Ella cantó entre lágrimas
por Paris por mí
la canción que confunde
una plegaria
con una mamada.

Así lo hacemos nosotros.
Este es mi tiempo.

LIKE A PRAYER

Back then I had a boyfriend
who would sing Madonna songs
and didn't know
if he wanted to be a drag queen
a poet or a meatpacker.

He was lacking talent
in almost all these trades
and others that flitted round
his greedy empty little head
asleep against my chest.

When Paris was attacked
on November thirteenth
Madonna was on tour
and my boyfriend had hit the road.

She sang through tears
for Paris for me
that song about
a prayer
or a blow job.

That's how we do it.
These are my times.

PEQUEÑO POEMA DE AUTOAYUDA

esta tarde
sentado en un banquito con las palabras cortas
vi pasar un camión de basura repleto
no pensé por supuesto
en el gobierno bolivariano
ni en los vertederos colapsados
y la ruina y las moscas y el hedor.

cuando pasó el camión de la basura
me dejó una metáfora muy linda:
así tenemos el corazón
repleto de tanto desecho tóxico
¿a dónde va el camión de la vida?
¿dónde verterá nuestros desvelos?
¿quién asea el estercolero
las caídas y los tropiezos del alma
de la llama violeta que arde?

y cómo voy a alegrarle la tarde
a algún lector mío
con este poema luminoso
ardido también
como la llama esa

voy a enderezarle los miedos
al lector mío   pobrecito
perdido por ahí carne de budismo
testigo potencial de Jehová
porque al fin no escribí
un poema quejumbroso
poema para poetas

LITTLE SELF-HELP POEM

this evening
sitting on a little bench and short on words
I saw a garbage truck go by full-up
I did not think of course
about the Bolivarian government
or trash dumps spilling over
and the ruin and the flies and stench.

when the garbage truck went by
it left a lovely little metaphor:
such are our hearts
full-up with so much toxic waste
where is our life's truck going?
where will it dump out our sleepless nights?
who spruces up the dunghill
the tumbles and totters of the soul
whose violet flame yet burns?

and how am I to brighten up the evening
of some reader of mine
with this gleaming poem
heated too
just like that flame

I shall settle the fears
of my poor little   reader
lost somewhere Buddhism fodder
potential witness of Jehovah
because in the end I did not write
a whiny poem
a poem for poets

y aquí lo tienes lector
calientito
para que dejes de hacer rico
a algún escritorzuelo extranjero
y me hagas rico a mí
      (escritorzuelo local)
que tuve toda la basura del mundo
apretada en el corazón
pero ya no lector
ya no.

and here you have it reader
nice and warm
so you stop making some foreign
hack writer rich
and start making a local hack writer
    (me) rich
I had all the trash in the world
crammed into my heart
but no longer dear reader
no longer.

TALLER DE POESÍA

se llamaba Yeison
o Mayker   el profesor
parecía un mendigo

entró al salón
de noche

y mirándome dijo

te voy a cortar la garganta

quisiera escribir un verso
de ese tamaño

lo he intentado
cientos de veces
y no consigo que el poema
toque así diga así
su propio límite

no consigo que el poema
haga lo que dice así
octosílabo castizo sinaléfico
eficaz.

POETRY WORKSHOP

the teacher's name
was Yeison   maybe Mayker
he looked like a beggar

he came in the classroom
at night

and looking at me said

I'll cut your throat

I'd like to write a line
that size

I've tried
hundreds of times
but can't get the poem
to touch to state
its own limit like that

I can't get the poem
to do what it says like that
polished dispondaic tetrasyllable:
effective.

LA LENGUA EN EL CULO: POÉTICA

1. El presidente de la república (o lo que queda de ella) ha bautizado "Chuquiluqui" al líder de la oposición (o lo que queda de ella). La precaria audacia versiona una vieja broma popular sobre un explorador perdido en la selva que, entre la muerte y el estupro, prefirió ser sodomizado. Lo gracioso es que ha debido elegir la muerte. Lo gracioso es que vale más un hombre muerto que un marico vivo.

2. El muchacho que protestaba en contra del gobierno y fue penetrado con un fusil por la Guardia Nacional Bolivariana no pudo elegir. Tampoco la policía permite a las transexuales, cada noche, decidir entre la muerte y la humillación. Pero acaso ellas lo tienen merecido. Eso decía un cartel de la Gobernación del Estado Carabobo: "Incitar al sexo produce violaciones". En tiempos de totalitarismo no hay lugar para las luchas menores.

3. Tiempos de totalitarismo y Nueva Era. Como una peste llegó de lejos nuestra pasión de vaciedad: un gato autista que araña el aire. No hay nada en el cielo, los astros y las señales cósmicas vienen del televisor. Cuando Saturno está en Acuario, la felicidad es una ley severa. Odiar no es cool. *Aborrecer es de mal gusto. El odio es la bandera de los perdedores y eso jamás.*

4. Lo correcto es callar: pensar que este país tiene problemas más importantes y violar a un muchacho que protesta es peor que violar a una prostituta (que ni siquiera es mujer). Callar: olvidar que tal vez un niño entendió el chiste del presidente. Callar: meterse la lengua donde desde hace tantos años está el fusil.

5. Pero yo (también) soy mi odio. Y escribo.

ARSE POETICA

1. The president of the republic (or what's left of it) has dubbed the leader of the opposition (or what's left of it) "Chuquiluqui." With this shaky boldness he adapts an often-told old joke about an explorer lost in the jungle who, forced to choose between death and buggery, chose to be sodomized. The funny part is he should have chosen death. The funny part is a dead man is worth more than a live faggot.

2. The young man who protested against the government and was penetrated with a rifle by the Bolivarian National Guard was not able to choose. Nor do the police allow transsexuals, every night, to decide between death and humiliation. But maybe they deserve it. A poster from the Carabobo State Government said: "Inciting Sex Causes Rape." In times of totalitarianism there is no place for minor struggles.

3. Times of totalitarianism and the New Age. Like a plague from afar came our passion for emptiness: an autistic lucky cat scratching the air. There is nothing in the sky, the stars and cosmic signs come from the TV screen. When Saturn is in Aquarius, happiness is law, strictly enforced. It is not cool to hate. Hatred is not in. Hatred is the flag of losers: never that.

4. The right thing to do is to be quiet: think this country has more important problems and raping a young man who protests is worse than raping a prostitute (who is not even a woman). Be quiet: forget maybe some little boy got the president's joke. Be quiet: stick your tongue in the place where the rifle has been all these years.

5. But I (too) am my hatred. And I write.

INSURGENT TEXTICLES
TEXTÍCULOS INSURRECTOS

I

ahora que las manos nos pertenecen
que otros osaron decir el nombre del amor que amamos
y hay ciudades enteras que nuestros abrazos no perturbarían
y buenas costumbres también para nosotros
y la vida no es noble ni buena ni sagrada para nadie.
ahora que tenemos un día como las madres y los trabajadores
que podemos dejar la estridencia a Ginsberg
la pornografía a Verlaine / la culpa a Lorca
la sublimación a Cernuda / los discursos a Lemebel.
ahora que no necesitamos ir a la cárcel ni a la marina ni al seminario
para tener a un hombre adentro.
quién se va a comer el cuento contado por siglos.
a quién le importa nuestro deseo ahora que está legalizado
lucífero público sano como el de ellos muerto.
Cómo decir después de Almodóvar de Cocteau
de Giorno de Barba Jacob y Gómez Jattin
que somos un nuevo rico escapando al fondo de la cámara dorada
para saborear subrepticiamente con sedición
harina de la infancia en el bruto paladar.

I

now that our hands belong to us
and others dare to call our love its name
and in whole cities we can hug and won't offend
and we have manners too
and life is neither good nor noble nor sacred for anyone.
now that we have a day like mothers and labor
and can leave garishness to Ginsberg
pornography to Verlaine / guilt to Lorca
sublimation to Cernuda / speeches to Lemebel.
now that we don't have to be in jail or the navy or seminary
to have a man inside us.
who will keep on eating up the story told for centuries.
who cares about our longing now it's legalized
illuminated public healthy dead like theirs.
How can we say after Almodóvar Cocteau
Giorno Barba-Jacob Gómez Jattin
we are nouveau riche escaping to the back of the treasure vault
whence to savor surreptitiously and in sedition
flour of youth on unrefined palates.

II

Toda sexualidad es heterosexual
a nadie seduce lo que es igual.
"Amaos los unos a los otros":
palabra de Dios.
Y aunque los otros reclamen
su derecho a amarse entre ellos
la nostalgia por los unos acecha.
Aceptémoslo: hay un hombre
corriente que nunca lograremos
tener.

II

All sexuality is heterosexual
sameness seduces no one.
"Love one another"
says the word of God.
But even while the others claim
their right to love amongst themselves
one's sick longing for someone lies in wait.
Let's face it: there's
a common man whom we will never
have.

III

a Gerardo Rosales

Papá, cuando sea grande
quiero ser pato.
Caminan raro, pero cómo nadan,
cómo se deslizan por la superficie
del lago, con qué gracia estoica
avanzan en línea hacia el matadero.

Papá, cuando sea grande
quiero ser mariposa.
Un gusano que vuela
nunca demasiado lejos
de las arañas.

Papá, cuando sea grande
quiero ser pargo.
No he visto uno vivo.
Pero fritos   son deliciosos.

Quiero ser algo jugoso y muerto
sobre la mesa del último banquete.

III

for Gerardo Rosales

Daddy, when I grow up
I want to be a pansy.
They might like the cold, but look how colorful
they are! Look how they take the shapes
of hearts and faces, and how gracefully
they wither as the earth dries up.

Daddy, when I grow up
I want to be a fairy,
flitting winged
on a diet of dust
until the last believer
loses faith in me.

Daddy, when I grow up
I want to be a queen:
to reign supreme
until   a blade takes off my head.

I want to be something pretty and dead
from the last storybook I'll ever read.

IV

Qué haremos con las cosas cuyo nombre ignoramos,
las cosas que aun mudas proyectan baba sobre los días.
Y qué haremos con lo mal escrito,
la rabia y el vértigo de naufragios:
el más tentador de los lugares comunes.
Qué haremos con el pasado y los muchachos
que no fueron tuyos y el sudor que regó la tierra
más dulce que el deseo. Qué haremos con el deseo,
cuando cansados ya de la mordaza florezca
en una boca diminuta, callada.
Quién será, entre todos, tu Ganímedes
y el mío   cuando nos demos por vencidos.

IV

What will we do with what we cannot name,
the mute things that drip drool onto our days.
And what will we do with the misprints,
the rage and vertigo of shipwrecks:
the most tempting cliché.
What will we do with the past and the boys
who weren't yours and the sweat that watered the earth
sweeter than lust. What will we do with lust
when, sick of the gag, it blooms
within a quiet little mouth.
Who, at last, will be your Ganymede
and mine   when we give up.

V

a Virgilio Piñera

los cangrejos no caminan para atrás
ni son inmortales

cualquiera puede tapar
el sol con un dedo

los últimos no lograrán
ser los primeros por eso
son los últimos

el tiempo no cura
todas las heridas

y nada en este mundo vale más
que cien pájaros volando libres
     en Guanabacoa.

V

for Virgilio Piñera

sharks aren't always moving
and are not a common cause of death

anyone can cover up
the sun with a finger

the last shall not
be first that's why
they're last

time does not heal
all wounds

and nothing in this world is worth more
than two birds free to nest together
       in one Guanabacoa bush.

VI

El niño de adentro es dador de fe
como una virgen de barro que llora sangre.
Perturbado quien lo mira teme
y porque teme cree.

El pequeño monstruo se acurruca
en la tiniebla porque sabe que no tiene
lo que da y lo necesita.
Y sabe que está mal amar con furia
lo que ama. Y sabe que si lo descubren
será para siempre solo para siempre
marcado para siempre roto.

Pero no puede evitarlo es un vicio
y se arrastra en la noche hasta otra cama
y mancha con su amor y mustia
lo que toca cuando nadie lo ve
y piensa que ha vencido porque
un cuerpo se estremece con su tacto
de muelas de leche y cada vez que todo
termina recuerda que está mal y jura no hacerlo
de nuevo y falla es un vicio.

Quiere ser un lagarto
poderoso   oler el peligro con la lengua.

VI

The little boy inside is a giver of faith
as if a clay Virgin crying blood.
Disturbed all who see him fear
and since they fear believe.

The little monster crouches
in the dark because he knows he doesn't have
what he gives and he needs it.
And he knows it's wrong to love fiercely
the thing he loves. And he knows if they find out
he'll forever be alone forever
marked forever broken.

But he cannot help it it's a vice
he drags himself at night up to another bed
and stains with love and withers
what he touches when no one is looking
and thinks he has won because
a body trembles at his milk-tooth
touch and every time it's all
over he remembers it is wrong and swears he won't do it
again and fails it is a vice.

He wants to be a mighty
lizard   smell danger on his tongue.

VII

La culpa es de los pollos.

Y qué genoma incompleto ni qué Edipo
ni qué sexo gonadal o desorden endocrino.

(Compadre no coma pollo)

VII

It's all soy's fault.

Don't give me
your incomplete genome your Oedipus
gonadal sex or endocrine disorder.

(Bro say no to soy)

VIII

Hay muchas formas de morir
y sobran los motivos.
La patria es una de las favoritas.
Dios   como quiera que se llame
el desconocido. Se puede morir al filo
de una espada en el acero de una bala
pendiendo de una soga se puede morir en vida
como Teresa como Virgilio.
Se puede vivir muriendo
como yo.

Y no importa la muerte es lo que nunca importa
apuesta segura el amigo en común
con todo enemigo el paraíso perdido poetas
lo único que no se puede cantar
la muerte enteramente libre / de baba.

Lo triste de morir es el motivo
cuando no acontece sin más cuando
vamos a su encuentro como niñas hombrunas
o adolescentes torcidos pensando que jamás
nadie nunca será capaz / de amarnos.

VIII

There are many ways to die
and far too many reasons to.
One's country is a favorite.
God   whatever you call
the unknown. You can die on the blade
of a sword on the sidewalk of a bullet
hanging from a noose you can die in life
like Teresa like Virgilio.
You can live dying
like me.

And it doesn't matter death never matters
safe bet mutual friend
with all our enemies paradise lost poets
the one thing that can't be sung
death absolutely free / of drool.

The sad part about dying is the reason
when it doesn't happen just because when
we go out to meet it like butch little girls
or bent teenagers thinking no one ever
never ever will know how / to love us.

IX

No recuerdo si quería un juguete
un helado o regresar a casa, insistí.
La respuesta, en cambio, no la olvido:
"más fastidioso que marico pidiendo beso".

Debí interpretar que insistir es malo
y ya sería bastante. La respuesta,
en cambio, me atrofió el deseo:
lo malo es pedir.

IX

I don't remember if I wanted a toy
an ice cream or to go back home, but I insisted.
The answer, though, I won't forget: an old saying.
"More annoying than a faggot asking for a kiss."

I should have got that insisting was wrong,
that's it. And yet the answer
atrophied my wishful heart:
it's wrong to ask.

X

el mariquito asexuado escucha
no tiene nada para contar
no le pasa nada

el mariquito asexuado es lo máximo
es mejor que la amiga gordita
no hay lipo para su lipa
y nadie lo prefiere

el mariquito asexuado no se queja
no llora aguanta
pide disculpas cuando lo ofenden
entiende
todos tienen problemas
necesitan ayuda
oídos ojos
el mariquito asexuado en cambio
no necesita nada

los feos creen que el mariquito asexuado
los ama en secreto
los bonitos con más razón
las mujeres creen que si no fuese marico
el mariquito asexuado las desposaría

a veces sueña un zarpazo el mariquito asexuado
pero no tiene zarpas
es inofensivo
dice lo que quieren escuchar
y asiente

X

the sexless homo listens
he has nothing to say
nothing is up with him

the sexless homo is the greatest
better than the plump girlfriend
there is no tuck to his tummy
and nobody likes him better

the sexless homo does not complain
he does not cry he bears it
he apologizes when he is offended
he understands
everyone has problems
needs help
ears eyes
the sexless homo on the other hand
needs nothing

ugly boys think the sexless homo
loves them secretly
pretty boys are right to think this
women think if he was not a homo
then the sexless homo would marry them

sometimes in his dreams the sexless homo sees
a long-clawed swipe striking a face
but he does not have claws
he's harmless
he says what they want to hear
and nods

es culpable de algo el mariquito asexuado
quién sabe
tal vez en otra vida fue malo
y ahora lo está pagando callado

cuántos amigos tiene el mariquito asexuado
es tan fácil hablar con él
sabe mucho de la vida
del amor y aunque es asexuado
sabe mucho de sexo el mariquito
sabe lo que complace a una mujer
alguna vez quiso ser mujer
sabe lo que complace a un hombre
es un hombre al fin

sabe todo de sí mismo
ah qué lúcido es el mariquito
qué perspicaz
sabe por ejemplo
que su vida será no lo gris
contra lo gris
menos todavía
no mucho.

is the sexless homo guilty of some crime
who knows
maybe he was wicked in another life
and now is paying for it quiet

see how many friends the sexless homo has
it's so easy to talk to him
he knows so much of life
of love and even though he's sexless
he knows so much about sex the homo
knows how to please a woman
once he wanted to be a woman
he knows how to please a man
after all he is a man

he knows all there is to know about himself
oh, how sensible the homo is
and how discerning
he knows for example
that his life will not be gray
on gray
but less than this
not much.

OÍDO EN LA CALLE

a David

—¿Cuál es tu peor temor?

—Llegar a viejo solo
y que un niño de quince años
me chulee.

OVERHEARD

for David

"What's your worst fear?"

"I grow old alone
and get played by
a fifteen-year-old boy."

MONSTRUATION
MONSTRUACIÓN

I

uno en realidad es más que uno
lo sabe bien   pero qué angustia

todo aquí dice yo y sin embargo
se agencia en mí una vieja pena

uno sueña que es uno   y no
es tan largo el yo   tan vago

se desparrama   equívoco
sin cuerpo que lo resista

las palabras se van con cualquiera
que pueda pagar su precio

cualquiera menos uno.

I

one really is more than oneself
one knows it well   but oh it hurts

all of this says I and yet
within myself an old sorrow is snagged

one dreams one is oneself   but isn't
the I so long   so vague

spills out   awry
no body to hold it back

words tag along with anyone
who can pay their price

anyone but oneself.

II

La vida espera
en algún sitio detrás
del dolor de tu madre.

Hay que merecer el aire
y la luz blanca del teatro.
Hay que merecer la agonía
de una mujer.

Y si te abren el camino
igual tendrás
que recorrerlo.

Sí, hasta algún sitio detrás
del dolor ajeno
donde la vida espera.

II

Life awaits
somewhere behind
your mother's pain.

You must deserve the air
the white light of the theater.
You must deserve the anguish
of a woman.

And if they pave a path for you
you will still have
to walk it.

Yes, all the way to someplace behind
the secondhand pain
where life awaits.

III

a Eleonora Cróquer

no soy capaz de decir siquiera
que no condeno
mi devaneo / prefiero las respuestas
todo lo quiero tener.

me hago la loca   pero soy un hombre
    qué vergüenza
tan bruto desesperado.

cuándo voy a aprender
a postergar el placer para que dure.

cuándo voy a aprender
a jugar con los huecos que no se pueden llenar.

III

for Eleonora Cróquer

I am incapable of even saying
I do not condemn
my dalliance / I prefer answers
I want to have everything.

I play the loca   but I am a man
        shame on me
a desperate brute.

when will I learn
to ration pleasure so it lasts.

when will I learn
to play with holes that can't be filled.

IV

Yo amo sólo mujeres defectuosas
estériles de vientre putas o poetas.
¿De qué sirve —en la guerra—
una mujer idiota una mujer mujer?
Colecciono cicatrices abortos persigo
una cabeza oscura paridora de versos
una infeliz que no haya querido
a sus hijos lúbrica baudeleriana lésbica mujer
incendiaria   libérrima.

IV

I love only malfunctioning women
barren-wombed or sluts or poets.
What's the use—in war—of
a dumb woman of a woman woman?
I hoard scars abortions I'm after
a dark head birthing verses
an unhappy girl who never loved
her kids lewd Baudelairean lesbian woman
starting fires   and wild.

V

Nací en una familia sin hombres
a pesar de tanto tío el padre
la testosterona tuve la suerte de nacer
escoltado por histéricas
de pelo en pecho.

V

I was born into a manless family
despite so many uncles dad
testosterone I got lucky was born
safeguarded by hysterics
with hair on their chests.

VI

Estoy absolutamente dispuesto a recordarle
a cada gordo negro judío feo
enano bruto viejo indio bizco
calvo zurdo pobre etcétera
y etcétera que compartimos bando.

Dadme un hombre
(las mujeres lo llevan por fuera)
y mi ojo entrenado para la ternura
señalará de qué margen está hecho.

¿Quién ha dicho que yo —y sólo
yo— soy diferente?

VI

I am absolutely willing to remind
the fat the Black the Jew the ugly
the dwarf the stupid the old the Indian the cross-eyed
the bald the left-handed the poor etcetera
and etcetera we are on the same team.

Give me a man
(women wear it on the outside)
and my well-trained eye for tenderness
will point to the margin he's made of.

Who said I—and only
I—was different?

VII

Cada año
(en Venezuela)
medio millón
de mujeres
aumentan el tamaño
de sus senos.

Así decimos aquí:
"este cuerpo
   es mío".

VII

Every year
(in Venezuela)
half a million
women
get
a boob job.

Here that's how we say:
"My body,
       my choice."

VIII

se-quiere-matar
matándo-se
se-quiere.

VIII

he-wants-to-kill-himself
he-loves-himself
killing-himself
he-wants-himself
he-loves-to-kill-himself.

IX

cuando los machos machotes
desenvainaron el látigo de la indiferencia
y me dejaron la espalda
imaginariamente rota
destrozada diría

juré que más nunca
que más
nunca
juré.

IX

when the machoest machos
cracked the whip of indifference
and left my back
imaginarily scourged
torn up I'd say

I swore never again
I never
swore
again.

LONELINESS GUTS
VÍSCERAS DE SOLEDADES

Like a stone on a sinking island.

Como una piedra sobre una isla que se hunde.

CÉSAR MORO

I

si ese amor no era más que sombra
del amor que había en mí
cómo podía ser bueno cómo podía
ser sino un racimo de vergüenzas

si amamos con el mismo amor
lo propio y lo ajeno confundidos
cómo no haberte ofrecido
la idéntica pasión que me dedico
a mí mismo: tu amor el que te di
desesperado por una víctima
en las antípodas de mi piel
era sombra de una sombra
nada más
una tregua con el espejo.

I

if that love was just the shadow
of the love there was in me
how could it be good how could it
be anything but a bouquet of shame

if we love with the same love
one's own and others' muddled up
how could I not have offered you
passion identical to what I give
myself: your love the love I gave you
desperate for a victim
at the antipodes of my skin
was shadow of a shadow
that is all
a truce with the mirror.

II

Cualquiera se equivoca
piensa que una palabra lo puede todo
y sólo hay que dar con ella: la sagrada
la canción de serenata el conjuro.
Prueba todas / a ver cuál es la correcta suplica
grita insiste y siente que tal vez
la próxima tal vez.

Pero nunca estuvimos tan lejos del amor
como cuando pensamos que casi lo logramos.

Con cuánta paciencia tuvimos que entender
renunciar a toda pretensión
y dejar que nos sorprenda

el brillo de lo que no será
la dignidad de lo que se entrega
sin más voluntad que la despojada
íngrima humildad de resto.

II

Everybody makes mistakes
thinks one word can do anything
and you just have to find it: sacred word
the song of serenade the summoning.
Try all of them / see which is right plead
scream insist and feel that maybe
next time maybe.

But we were never so far from love
as when we thought we'd almost made it.

How much patience did it take for us to understand
give up on all pretension
and let ourselves be surprised

by the shine of what will not be
the dignity of what is handed over
with no will beyond the dispossessed
forsaken humbleness of what's left.

III

a Rafael Castillo Zapata

No escribiré un soneto sobre tus doradas hebras
ni contaré en secreto los lunares de tu espalda

para que el tiempo haga su trabajo.

Lo único que estoy dispuesto a contar
son los días que le quedan a tu hechizo.

Voy a sentarme a mirar cómo envejeces
voy a sabotear el poema   no escribiré
el Housman que esperabas. Tampoco
el Biedma que yo no sé darte.

Tu cuerpo sólo me tiene a mí
entre todos los artífices del canto

el que prefiere desentonar tu bolero   furioso.

III

for Rafael Castillo Zapata

I will not write a sonnet on your gilded locks
nor will I count unseen the freckles on your back

that time might do his work.

The only thing I am willing to count:
the days your spell has left.

I'm going to take a seat to watch you age
I'm going to sabotage the poem   I won't write
the Housman you hoped for. Nor
the Biedma I can't give you.

Out of all the artisans of song
your body has me only

me angry who'd rather sing your ballad   out of tune.

IV

Para ver el cielo en las paredes no necesitabas
más que un poco de hierba crecida en los confines
de un mundo hecho ruinas en el advenimiento
de la soledad.

Pero no quise las hierbas y
veía paredes en las paredes.

¿Dónde estabas cuando supe al fin
que yo sostenía la daga?
¿Por qué has venido tan sólo
para llamarme puta y fea?

Te mentí.

Dejé que pensaras que podía ver
lo que habías inventado para alguien más.
Pero nada de cielo
quiero decirlo ahora: descolorida pared.

IV

To see heaven on the walls you needed nothing
but a little grass grown at the edges
of a world made ruins at the advent
of solitude.

But I turned down the grass and
saw walls on the walls.

Where were you when I finally realized
the dagger was in my hand?
Why did you come only
to call me ugly and a whore?

I lied to you.

I let you think I could see
what you made up for someone else.
But there was no heaven
I want to tell you: dingy old wall.

V

no, no iré jamás al psicoanalista
soy débil.

lo único que me falta   (el colmo)
es pagar por estar enamorado
sin ninguna esperanza.

V

no, I will never go to a therapist
I'm weak.

the last thing I need   (to top it off)
is to be hopelessly in love
and pay for it.

VI

Voy a meterle mano a este poema.
Voy a lamerlo, voy a mentirle, voy a perder
la cabeza por este poema como si fuese
un hombre.
Voy a mirarle los pies largamente,
voy a mirarle el paquete a este poema como
si fuese de carne.
Ignoraré las señales de alerta, no podré
decidir si es amor o deseo o hastío lo que
me arrodilla frente a este poema.
Y no alzaré la mirada hasta su corazón:
me gusta el poema de la cintura para abajo.
Este poema no tiene corazón y el mío
a esta hora es del muchacho que exprime las naranjas.

VI

I will feel this poem up.
I will lick it, lie to it, lose
my head over this poem like it was
a man.
I will stare at its feet,
check out this poem's package as
if it were flesh.
I will ignore the warning signs, won't know
if it is love or lust or boredom
bringing me down to my knees before this poem.
And I will not look up at its heart:
I like this poem waist-down.
This poem has no heart and mine belongs
for now to the boy at the orange stand
juicing.

VII

Cuando llegue Antonio vamos a exigirle
que nos llene la boca con su lengua
a cambio del poema.

El milagro no será su gacela
sin cuerpo. Vamos a meter el dedo
en las cuatro llagas para que entienda.

¿Qué se ha creído la belleza?

Ya no le tenemos miedo.

Si no coopera yo diré su secreto:
no fueron los dioses ni el caballo,
la caída de Troya fue culpa de Helena.

VII

When Antonio gets here we'll demand
he fill our mouths with his tongue
in exchange for the poem.

The miracle will not be his bodiless
gazelle. We'll stick our finger
in the four wounds so he understands.

What does beauty think it is?

We don't fear it anymore.

If it doesn't play along I'll tell its secret:
it was neither gods nor horse,
the fall of Troy was Helen's fault.

VIII

Mírame ya no puedo equivocarme
soy invencible.

A ti voy a quererte como Gorgona
la mujer florecida de veneno
que por venganza convertía hombres
en cosas.

VIII

Look at me I can be wrong no more
I am invincible.

And you I will love with Medusa's love
the woman bloomed in venom
who in vengeance turns men
into things.

IX

entonces / así es como se siente

como despertar sudando desconsuelo
saber que era sueño   y seguir sudando

como pasear sobre cadáveres frescos
ocultando el horror de la victoria

así es como se siente entonces
ser amado.

IX

so / this is how it feels

like waking up sweating sorrow
knowing it was all a dream   but still sweating

like strolling over fresh corpses
hiding the horror of victory

so this is what it feels like
to be loved.

X

Narciso
me miró un día
tan intensamente
que sentí mi corazón
galopar por todo el cuerpo
buscando un hueco
para salir y entregarse.

Pero se miraba a sí mismo
Narciso
se miraba en mis ojos.

La sonrisa más bella del mundo
la sonrisa del millón de dólares
años de jalonear los dientes
y apretarlos y químicos
que los hicieran blancos
para qué
la sonrisa más bella del mundo
sin estrenar.

Yo no lo maté,
él se ahogó
en mis ojos.

X

Narcissus
looked me so deep
in the eyes one day
I felt my heart
gallop around inside my body
seeking a hole
through which
to give itself to him.

But he was looking at himself
Narcissus
saw Narcissus in my eyes.

The world's prettiest smile
the million-dollar smile
years of shifting teeth
and squeezing them
and whitening chemicals
for what
the world's prettiest smile
unworn.

I did not kill him,
he drowned
in my eyes.

XI

él es una fuerza de la naturaleza
la tormenta perfecta
en la costa adriática
él se desnuda canta se despeina
hace y dice lo que le da la gana
y siempre gana y corre
él es una tromba de versos
un cazador de trinitarias
él está en peligro de extinción
ya no hay hombres como él
galácticos ni poetas
ni canciones ni arrabales
él es un seísmo
de quinientos grados
en la escala del deseo
su boca está derritiendo
el casquete polar
su boca hizo llover en Somalia
en su boca el mundo se acaba
su boca munda el mundo
su boca que no muda
ni enmudece ni se inmunda
ni termina
tiene la boca en los ojos
tiene los ojos más grandes que la boca
él muerde con los ojos
pide a dios que le cuide el sufrimiento
se zambulle y corre
tiene la lengua más grande que los ojos
tiene la lengua destrozada de tanto decir sí
tiene la lengua metida en el centro de la tierra
él ha desmantelado el Golfo de Tarento

XI

he is a force of nature
the perfect storm
on the Adriatic coast
he gets naked sings musses his hair
makes and says whatever he wants
and always wins and comes
he is a flux of verses
a hunter of wildflowers
he is endangered
there are no men like him anymore
galactic men no poets
no songs no slums
he is a magnitude five hundred
earthquake
on the scale of lust
his mouth is melting
the polar ice cap
his mouth made it rain in Somalia
in his mouth the world ends
his mouth worlds the world
his mouth whose words
are unceasing undirty undone
his mouth is in his eyes
his eyes are bigger than his mouth
he bites with his eyes
he asks god to protect his suffering
he dives and comes
his tongue is bigger than his eyes
his tongue is torn up he says yes so much
his tongue is stuck into the center of the earth
he has dismantled the Gulf of Taranto
with a stroke

de una caricia
él tiene lunares imposibles
lunares minerales
mariposas en la lengua
él preferiría no hacerlo
pero masturba ballenas
huele mis zapatos
y llora y corre
él duele
no como duele la belleza
sino como duele la libertad
él arde
mar en la herida
él controla la marea
él es puro piedra pura
piedra dura y magma y todo
él está enamorado
de sí mismo
tiene hambre de audiencia
y llora y corre
y dice que no sabe pero sabe
no le importa
él grita los orgasmos y corre
parece que viene
pero se va.

he has unreal freckles
mineral freckles
butterflies on his tongue
he would prefer not to
but he jerks off whales
smells my shoes
and cries and comes
he hurts
not like beauty hurts
but like freedom hurts
he burns
sea in the wound
he handles the tide
he is pure stone pure
hard stone and magma and everything
he is in love
with himself
he is hungry for an audience
and cries and comes
and says he doesn't know but he knows
he doesn't care
he screams his orgasms and comes
he looks like he's about to take
the plunge off the cliff
but he is only
edging.

(NOVELITA FAMILIAR IMAGINARIA)

1. El abuelo

El viejo lo llevaba en hombros
por la playa mientras contaba historias.
Con voz ronca decía: De la gracia de Dios,
         niño, sólo nos queda el mar.

Su sexo endurecía
contra la nuca del abuelo,
la blanca cabeza entre sus piernas.

El anciano lo sabía y cada tarde
lo llevaba en hombros por la playa:

Si yo te amara,   niño,
metería tu cabeza pequeña
en el agua. Mi cabeza y tu cabeza
en el agua, si me amara,
si no tuviera tanto miedo
de los ojos de Dios,
escrutándome.

Y el niño le abrazaba de muslos
el cuello fláccido con fuerza.

(LITTLE MADE-UP FAMILY NOVEL)

1. Grandpa

The old man bore him on his shoulders
down the beach and told him stories.
Hoarse-voiced, he'd say: All we have left
    of God's grace, my boy, is the sea.

His penis would harden
at the nape of Grandpa's neck,
white hair between his legs.

The old man knew and every afternoon
he bore him on his shoulders down the beach:

If I loved you,   my boy,
I'd hold your little head
under the water. My head and your head
under the water, if I loved myself,
if I were not so scared
of God's eyes
looking down on me.

And the boy would squeeze his thighs
tighter around his flaccid neck.

2. *El salvavidas*

Prohibido nadar,
decía el cartel.
Y junto a él un muchacho
prohibido, como el mar.

¿Por qué parece un ángel?
Preguntó el niño
a su madre.

Ella cerró la Biblia en la que
dormitaba. Tenía ocho años
sin saber lo que es un hombre,
ocho años sola, durmiendo
con un niño seca.

Le dijo: Las caricias del mar
               ponen el cuerpo duro.

Y escuchó el agua revuelta.
Así ha de ser el infierno,
pensó la madre con los ojos
apretados.

Así ha de ser el infierno,
pensó el niño
que miraba al muchacho
todavía.

2. Lifeguard

No swimming,
said the sign.
And beside it a young man
just like the sea, forbidden.

Why does he look like an angel?
The boy asked
his mother.

She closed the Bible in which she
was dozing off. Eight years had passed
since she had known a man,
eight years alone, sleeping
dry beside a little boy.

She told him: *The touch of the sea*
                     chisels the body.

And she listened to the choppy water.
This is hell,
the mother thought with eyes
closed tight.

This is hell,
the boy thought
looking at the young man
still.

3. Conversación con el abuelo

La bendición, abuelo.
Debes estar cansado.
Yo también lo estoy
aunque no tengo derecho.
Es largo, ¿verdad?
El camino, digo.
Ayer por la mañana
en el puente me detuve
quería saltar.
No supe de pronto
qué había del otro lado
ya sé que vivir sin más
y después ser como tú
que sabes tantas cosas.
Y no era eso, abuelo,
lo que yo no sabía.
No sabía por qué
ir al otro lado.
Supongo que todos
alguna vez
sentimos eso al cruzar
un puente.
Pero algo saltó esa mañana.

Jura que no repetirás
esto: hay un perro
en la escuela.
Y hoy,
sin ningún motivo,
cuando nadie miraba,
le hice daño.
Lo levanté del suelo
a patadas.

3. Conversation with Grandpa

Bless me, Grandpa.
You must be tired.
I'm tired too
although I have no right to be.
Long, isn't it?
The road, I mean.
Yesterday morning
I stopped at the bridge
wanting to jump off.
All of a sudden
I didn't know what
was on the other side
I know just living
and then being like you
who knows so many things.
But that's not it, Grandpa,
what I didn't know.
I didn't know why I'd
go to the other side.
I guess we all
sometimes
feel that way when we cross
a bridge.
But that morning something jumped off.

Swear you won't repeat
this: there's a dog
at school.
And today,
for no reason,
when no one was looking,
I hurt him.
I kicked him so hard he

Tiré de su lomo
hasta escucharlo gritar.
Hay algo que espanta
en el dolor de un animal,
pero seguía haciéndolo,
abuelo.
No podía creer
que siguiera moviéndome
la cola,
que siguiera amándome.

¿Cómo puedo
no ser esclavo
de mi cuerpo?
¿Por qué debo llevarlo
con toda su maldad
al otro lado de los puentes?

Hoy la maestra pidió
que le contáramos
un sueño.
Yo sólo tengo pesadillas
una y otra vez
la misma.
¿Sabes lo que es, abuelo
una pesadilla?
Es un sueño
que no se puede contar.
La anécdota sí, claro,
pero el terror,
el terror no.
Entonces no dije nada
porque para qué.
Y la maestra me odia.

jumped into the air.
Pulled on his tail
until I heard him yelp.
There's something scary
in an animal's pain,
but I kept doing it,
Grandpa.
I couldn't believe
he kept wagging his tail
at me,
he kept on loving me.

How can I
not be
my body's slave?
Why must I carry it
and all its evil
across bridges?
Today our teacher asked
us to tell her
a dream.
I only have nightmares
over and over
the same one.
Grandpa, do you know what
a nightmare is?
A dream
you cannot tell.
What happens in it you can, of course,
but not the terror, not
the terror, no.
So I said nothing.
Why would I?
The teacher hates me.

ON TRANSLATING *WILD WEST*

I have never been to Caracas. Much less have I been to the Caracas that Alejandro Castro depicts in *El lejano oeste*: the city's swelling, decadent west side, where life is often cheap and lifestyles are defined by the logic of the streets. I have never been held at knifepoint after a poetry class, or been shunned by society for loving the wrong person, or heard the sound of size-twelve heels clacking down Avenida Libertador.

I have lived a life of ease and privilege. My parents are well-educated professionals from England, and I was born and raised in the perfectly central US state of Oklahoma, where I still live today. My knowledge of the Spanish language, and of Spanish-language literature, was largely acquired in the classroom. I first encountered Venezuelan poetry in a textbook, not in an alleyway.

So what would happen if I found myself, like the little avatar from Google Earth, plucked up and dropped into Alejandro's Caracas? How would I come to terms with these new surroundings?

This is the question I asked myself when my friend Garcilaso Pumar, bold leader of Alliteration Publishing, asked me to translate *El lejano oeste*. I read the book, found it enthralling, and thought: this project will chew me up and spit me out. How could I—a sheltered, scholarly, relatively straight guy from a relatively podunk state—translate a book so brutal, so bitter, so urban, and so vehemently queer?

I had no answer, but translation is always a game of impossibilities. So I started working, as one must, and predictably I found myself feeling like what I was: something of an idiot abroad, a tourist getting turned around and misreading the street signs, missing points, obscuring meanings, more intruder than interpreter. With time and toil I completed a passable draft of the book in this fashion, but I knew I would need a trusty guide to get it to its final destination.

That's where Alejandro came in. We sadly missed each other when I visited New York City for the Brooklyn Book Festival (and for the first time) in September of 2022, before my first draft of *Wild West* was complete. We ended up connecting via Zoom later that fall, and then meeting regularly over the course of several months, talking bit by bit about every single poem and then doing it all over again. As our conversations progressed, ducks became pansies, crabs became sharks, breast enlargements became boob jobs, and running became coming; oranges were juiced and punctuation marks erased; and author and translator turned from strangers into friends.

Alejandro taught me a master class in *caraqueño* diction and queer semiotics, always generous with his comments and accepting of his poems' inevitable metamorphoses as they moved into English. He was patient with my often scholarly inquiries and my often flowery first instincts, and together, we coaxed the rarefied language of my first draft into something cruel, grimy, uncommon, and beautiful: a book that hits in English, pulls no punches, and—I hope—does justice to its origins.

I will always be grateful to Alejandro for taking me by the hand, leading me through streets I never thought I'd know, guiding me to diamonds in the rough, and welcoming me into his world.

This book's last poem asks: why bother bearing our weight over bridges? Is the effort demanded by this act of survival really worth it? If Alejandro will permit me one last highbrow innuendo: the English word *translate* is cognate with the Spanish *trasladar* from the Latin *translatus*, "carried across." These poems were well worth carrying across, and I'm honored to have helped them reach the other side.

Arthur Malcolm Dixon

NOTES

SONG FOR BOLÍVAR (p. 31). This poem's reference to "bo-chinche" alludes to a famous statement by Francisco de Miranda, the father of Venezuelan independence, upon his arrest by Simón Bolívar and other revolutionaries who considered him a traitor to their cause.

SPELLING (p. 49). In Spanish, the letters *v* and *b* sound identical. It is therefore easy to confuse the spelling of the words *votar* (to vote) and *botar* (to throw away, to toss out, to litter). Here, the phrase *prohibido botar basura* ("no littering" or "no throwing out trash") is misspelled as *prohibido votar basura* ("no voting for trash").

FUNCTION OF POETRY (p. 67). The final lines of this poem play with the polysemy of the author's name. *Alejo* is both a nickname for "Alejandro" and the first-person present-tense conjugation of the verb *alejar* (to move away, to get away, to distance). Similarly, *castro* is the first-person present-tense conjugation of the verb *castrar* (to castrate).

V (p. 95). In Virgilio Piñera's native Cuba, a *pájaro* (bird) is an effeminate gay man.

III (p. 117). This poem makes reference to the figure of the *loca*. In Venezuela and elsewhere in Latin America, the term *loca*, literally "madwoman," also refers to an effeminate gay man.

INDEX

WILD WEST | ALEJANDRO CASTRO

Made in Miami Beach ~ Printing as needed

◊◊◊

2023

www.ingramcontent.com/pod-product-compliance
Lightning Source LLC
Chambersburg PA
CBHW020158090426
42734CB00008B/866